# FORTS & CASTLES

## MASTERPIECES OF ARCHITECTURE

### Terri Hardin

**TODTRI**

This book was designed and produced by ·
TODTRI Book Publishers
P.O. Box 572, New York, NY 10116-0572
FAX : (212) 695-6984
e-mail : info@todtri.com


*Printed and bound in Indonesia by APP Printing*


ISBN 1-57717-032-6


*Author:* Terri Hardin

*Publisher:* Robert M. Tod
*Editorial Director:* Elizabeth Loonan
*Book Designer:* Mark Weinberg
*Senior Editor:* Cynthia Sternau
*Project Editor:* Ann Kirby
*Photo Editor:* Edward Douglas
*Picture Researchers:* Meiers Tambeau, Laura Wyss
*Production Coordinator:* Jay Weiser
*Desktop Associate:* Paul Kachur
*Typesetting:* Command-O Design


Visit us on the web!
www.todtri.com

## PICTURE CREDITS

**Art Resource, New York**
Giraudon 39
Erich Lessing 48, 49, 54 (top & bottom), 55
Scala 69

**Corbis-Bettmann**
64, 68, 75

**Mary Evans Picture Library**
16 (bottom), 18 (bottom left), 21 (top), 22, 35, 47 (top)

**Robert Fried**
8–9, 24–25, 59, 61 (top & bottom)

**The Image Works**
Richard Dean 66–67
Esbin-Anderson 29
The Image Works Archives 52 (top)
Michael Justice 50–51 (top)
Salaber 31
Lee Snider 42 (bottom), 52 (bottom), 65 (top & bottom), 71, 72–73

**The Library of Congress, Washington, D.C.**
70

**Buddy Mays Travel Stock**
10–11

**Patti McConville & Les Sumner**
78–79

**New England Stock Photo**
Michael J. Howell 16 (top), 38
Jim Schwabel 63

**The Picture Cube**
David Ball 26
Glasheen Graphics 45

**Picture Perfect**
18–19, 23, 53 (top)
Peter Bastaja 27 (top), 32, 33 (top), 36, 46, 53 (bottom)
Charles Bowman 34
Dave & Les Jacobs 44
Allan Montaine 56–57
Nawrocki Stock Photo 5, 40–41, 42 (top), 43, 76–77
Jack Olsen 47 (bottom), 51 (bottom)
E. Simanor 7
C.T.H. Smith 13
R. Thompson 33 (bottom)

**Private Collection**
14 (left), 18 (top left)

**Topham/The Image Works**
14–15, 20, 30

**Nik Wheeler**
21 (bottom), 60, 62 (top & bottom)

**Woodfin Camp & Associates**
Jonathan Blair 37
Timothy Eagan 17
Robert Frerck 12, 28
Stephanie Maze 58
William Strode 74
Baron Wolman 6 (top & bottom)
Adam Woolfit 27 (bottom)

# CONTENTS

# INTRODUCTION

The instinct for defense is part of the instinct for survival. It is a primal instinct that we share with animals, but in humans it manifests itself in several art forms. Over the course of human history, the need for defense has often spurred as much (and perhaps even more) creative energy and resourcefulness as the desire for beauty or wealth.

For centuries, the greatest representations of the survival instinct have been military or defensive fortifications, such as strong walls or fortresses. In ancient times, the castle in particular was a magnificent show of strength. The success of a castle lay in its ability to withstand hostile forces, to break them with its unyielding might. Such a structure would be the envy of its enemies; it would be copied, refined, and embellished as technological innovations presented themselves.

This book will demonstrate how military architecture such as castles and other fortifications evolved as the forces that made them vied for supremacy.

In the beginning, humans—like other animals—sought defensive refuges in nature. These were found in mountains or other promontories, as well as in caves and natural borders such as cliffs or coastlines. Perhaps not surprisingly, such places were often revered as the abodes of gods and other supernatural forces, since their locations granted a measure of security. Even now, we try to build manmade fortifications that also incorporate natural defenses.

In time, it was discovered that naturally defensible areas could be improved upon by building up or enhancing their natural characteristics—for example, by raising walls, digging ditches or moats, or by changing the course of waterways and otherwise breaking up the landscape. These enhancements made it more difficult to traverse the area (and, therefore, to attack it).

Walls were perhaps the first substantial defense structure. Defensive walls have appeared in a variety of forms throughout the world, and serve as testaments to human ingenuity. The earliest of these were no doubt made by moving earth and building with stones.

RIGHT: Though it no longer serves the purpose for which it was built, Belem Tower in Lisbon, Portugal, like many fortresses, stands as a symbol of national pride and its country's rich history.

**RIGHT:** First fortified in the first or second century B.C., Masada was further strengthened under Herod the Great by the addition of two grand palaces, aqueducts, a bathhouse, and siege walls.

**BELOW:** Masada is a mountaintop fortress that sits 1,300 feet (397 meters) above the Dead Sea. Its defenses were so strong that one thousand Jewish defenders held off a force of fifteen thousand Romans for two years. They were overcome in A.D. 73, finally committing mass suicide rather than allowing themselves to be captured.

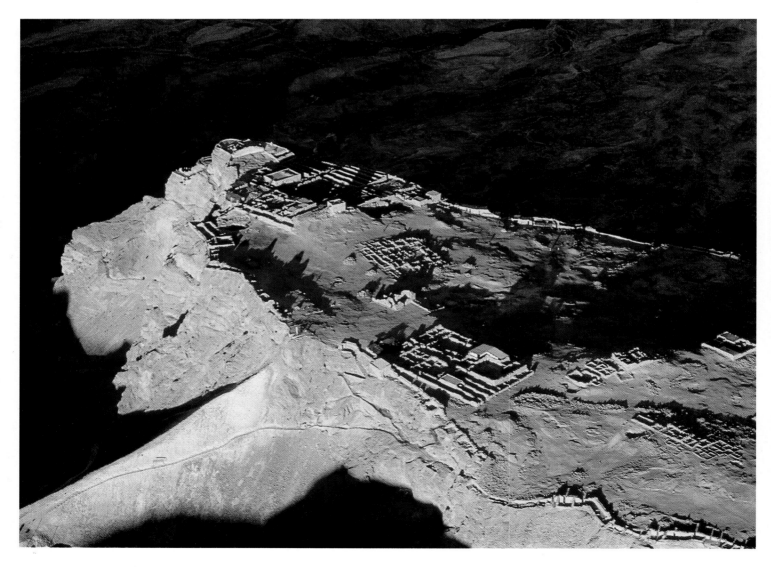

The Bible has been a reliable source for the history of the ancient empires such as Egypt, Babylon, and Mesopotamia that grew around the Nile, Tigris, and Euphrates rivers. Many ruins of their ancient cities exist, and these display the remains of the fortified walls that once surrounded them. Included among these is the Median Wall of Mesopotamia as well as the Ishtar Gate (c. 600 B.C.), which formed part of the city wall of Babylon. Around the seventh century B.C., it is recorded that Nabopolasser and his son, Nebuchadnezzar, rebuilt the city. The Ishtar Gate is among the sights recorded by Herodotus, the early Greek traveler and historian who wrote of his visit to Babylon in the fifth century B.C.

*Forts & Castles* will explore the fascinating rise and evolution of military defenses through the course of history, from the palisaded encampments used by Roman legions, to the stone battlements of the middle ages, to the frontier outposts of the Colonial period.

**ABOVE:** The origin of Jerusalem's wall may go back as far as 2,000 years, but the current walls of Jerusalem near the Jaffa Gate were rebuilt by Suleiman the Magnificent in the sixteenth century.

**FOLLOWING PAGE:** The massive stone walls crafted by the Inca, as seen here at Cuzco, Peru, were precisely cut and fitted together without mortar. Masterful pieces of defensive architecture that they were, they failed to withstand the Conquistadors.

# CHAPTER ONE

# THE ANCIENT WORLD

In western history, one of the most legendary early fortified cities we know of is Troy, thanks primarily to the poet Homer. In Homer's *Iliad*, Troy is a mighty city besieged by the Achaians, a league of Greek nations. The leader of the Achaians was Agamemnon, the king of Mycenae.

For centuries, both Troy and Mycenae were believed to be the stuff of legend. In 1870, however, Troy's existence was confirmed by the archaeologist Heinrich Schliemann (1822–90). Schliemann had been attracted to archaeology through his passion for Homer's *Iliad* and other great legends. Together with his wife (a Greek citizen), who served as translator, and a copy of the *Iliad* as a guidebook, Schliemann uncovered site after site of antiquity, enriching civilization (and himself) with treasures in the process.

Not every ancient culture built fortifications. The Minoans, who lived on the island of Crete, did not ring their palaces and cities with walls but seemed to prefer the natural defense of the

LEFT: The glory of Mycenae was destroyed in the fifth century B.C., and forgotten until its discovery in the late nineteenth century by the father of archaeology, Heinrich Schliemann. Here are seen the foundations of fortifications, which indicate a round tower protected by an encircling stone wall.

sea. The Mycenaeans, who subsequently conquered the Minoans and absorbed Minoan culture into their own, took a different view. Magnificent remains of Mycenaean culture were also uncovered by Schliemann. These include such Bronze Age fortifications as the famous Lion's Gate (1250 B.C.).

## Defensive Walls

In the fifth century B.C., Periclean Athens was protected by the wall of the Piraeus, which stretched from the harbor to the city and was the city's first defense. Other walls included the antique "cyclopean" walls found in the Spanish countryside of Cartagena and Taragonna. Spain, the portion of the European mainland closest to Africa, was frequently invaded throughout antiquity and retained a great many remnants of ancient cultures.

Of all the famous walls of antiquity, none comes close in scope to the Great Wall of China. Originating in the third century B.C., this lasting achievement of the C'hin dynasty (221–206 B.C.) can even be seen from outer space. The Great Wall spans 1,500 miles (2,414 kilometers) of China's northern border. It was originally made up of walls protecting individual states, but these were joined to form a single wall as the emperor Huang-ti gradually unified China.

As with other fortifications, the Great Wall was intended to keep invaders out. It succeeded in doing so until the fourteenth century, when it was breached by the invading Manchus. Today, tourists are able to walk along the wall, which ranges from 13 to 40 feet (4 to 12 meters) wide and rises between 20 to 50 feet (6 to 15 meters) from the ground. They can also view the

ABOVE: The famous Lion's Gate, symbol of the royal house of Atreus, was uncovered by Heinrich Schliemann in 1874. The gate itself dates to the thirteenth century B.C.

RIGHT: About 90 miles (145 kilometers) south of Beijing, the Great Wall of China seems to meander across the countryside. In truth, it was originally not one but several walls, which were joined together by the Emperor Huang-ti in the third century B.C. and renovated in the fifteenth century under the Ming dynasty.

**BELOW:** In this illustration the Western Gate of Beijing is seen as it must have appeared in the nineteenth century. City gates were often the most important for both trade and defense, and so were the best fortified.

renovations and embellishments added at the time of the Ming dynasty (1368–1644).

Although it is the largest structure in the Far East (and in the world), the Great Wall was not the only fortification of its kind. Imitations have been found throughout Asia, particularly in Korea and Japan. At first, the Japanese relied on the seacoast to ward off invaders, later raising crude bulwarks of earth to fend off the indigenous Ainu. In the centuries before the Japanese government was reorganized under an emperor (during the Taika Reformation, c. 645 A.D.), stone forts (*kogo-ishi*) were built and reinforced caves (*chiyash*i) constructed. Neither of these were intended for dwelling. In the course of time, the Japanese refined their fortifications using both Chinese and European models.

Also in the fifth century B.C., the city of Persepolis, in present-day Iran, was a jewel of the once-mighty Persian Empire and the seat of the famous Darian dynasty. A wall can be still be seen there with a detailed bas-relief depicting the Empire in its greatness. The dynasty fell into disarray in the fourth century B.C., when it was conquered by Alexander the Great (330 B.C.).

**RIGHT:** Instead of encircling their cities with walls, the ancient Greeks often built an elevated citadel in which citizens could find shelter from attack. Here, the acropolis of Corinth—the Acrocorinth—is seen looming high over the ruins of a temple to Apollo.

**ABOVE:** Completed in 1099 and built on the remains of existing Roman walls, the military encampment of Avila consisted of eighty-eight rounded towers connected by a high stone curtain wall.

**RIGHT:** This fortress, supposedly protected by a water barrier, proves vulnerable to a Roman siege tower ingeniously mounted on a raft of eight ships lashed together.

Although he hailed from the wild northern land of Macedonia and thus cannot be considered classically Greek, Alexander was still a devoted Hellene who sought to instill the Greek ideal in all his conquests. Enforcing both military and civil architecture in the Grecian style was one way of implementing Hellenistic culture. Alexander's empire, however, collapsed quickly upon his death. The conquerors who had the greatest lasting influence—even to this day—are the Romans.

It is hard to walk where Romans traveled and not find stoneworks for every municipal purpose. There are Roman baths in Corinth, Roman aqueducts throughout Italy, Roman temples in France, and Roman roads in Britain—to name just a few examples. Most prevalent are Roman military fortifications, because the Romans built defensive structures in all of their conquered territories.

**BELOW:** This reconstruction of a Bronze Age fortified dwelling in Ireland has several features of later castles: a defensive wall, a gate surmounted by a watch tower, and a water barrier.

## The Beginnings of the Castle

To this day, Roman fortresses still circumscribe what were the earliest bounds of Western civilization. Roman legions traversed the ancient world with superb military discipline, and wherever they stopped they would build a defensible military encampment. The longer they stayed, the more they shored up their defenses; at first with timber (if available) and earthworks, and later with stone. It is from the Latin term for these camps, *castellum*, that the word "castle" is derived.

Long after the Roman Empire collapsed and the far lands of England were repopulated with nomadic tribes, Roman edifices were regarded with awe, and sometimes considered to be the work of giants and warlocks. But it was also recognized that the Romans had been experts at detecting and reinforcing natural strategic points and, for this reason, many castle foundations were laid on old Roman fortress sites.

The Romans were as expert at attack as they were at defense. As early as the fourth century, they invented neuro-ballistic machines that could lay waste to fortifications. In addition to these, the Romans also developed an arsenal of siege machines, including the ballista, the catapult, siege towers, and the battering ram.

**BELOW:** The destruction of the Temple of Jerusalem by the Romans in A.D. 70 was a seminal moment in Western history. This nineteenth-century illustration, however, depicts the event as occurring in the quadrangular fortress plan that became popular many centuries later.

**ABOVE:** A Roman force uses the oldest of siege weapons, the battering ram, to attack the weakest structural point of a stone fort, its wooden gate. The men propelling the ram are protected by a sturdy wooden housing.

**RIGHT:** The Romans were among the first Europeans to recognize the importance of defensive structures, which they built to last. In the north of England, at what was the western limit of the Empire, the Wall of Hadrian can still be found, eighteen centuries after its creation.

**ABOVE:** Ancient Byzantium, later called Constantinople, was seemingly impregnable, protected by triple walls of massive towers and fortifications. Despite all these defenses, the city was taken by invaders on three occasions.

Many of these weapons faded from use with the decline of the Roman Empire and were reintroduced as castles again became a popular way to challenge the wits of prospective besiegers.

# The Byzantine Empire

As inheritors of the great Roman legacy, the Byzantines built many great fortifications throughout their empire. These included the early-tenth-century palace of Constantine Porphyrogenitus and the fourth-century Theodosian Wall, both in Asia Minor (present-day Turkey).

While fortifications and defensive enclosures as such had existed for centuries, the design of the classic medieval castle actually originated in Asia Minor in the sixth and seventh centuries. Under continuous attack from various hostile peoples on a number of fronts, the Byzantines created a temporary defensive structure made of timber and earthworks. This structure offered quick cover and a position from which to retaliate. The design was envied and quickly adapted by the Moslems, who were superb engineers, as evidenced by the Palace of Isa Ibn Musa (c. 774 A.D.) in Ukheidur, near Baghdad in present-day Iraq.

The Moslems thoroughly refined the design of the castle, and by the tenth century, it was they who were the masters of military architecture—and the castle. (The type of ornamentation derived from these castles—a combination of European and Oriental motifs—is called *mudejar*.)

**LEFT:** Assyrian soldiers, using scaling ladders, pour over the walls to seize a castle. No stronghold, however well designed and built, was completely secure from a determined and well-disciplined foe.

**ABOVE:** At a time when Europeans were relying upon wooden strongholds, advanced stone structures were built in the Middle East, such as this eighth-century castle in present-day Iraq.

Es nouuelles dalbyon
Sil vous en plaist escouter
mon frere z mon compaignon

## CHAPTER TWO

# THE OLD WORLD

The first castles of Europe, built around the ninth century, were of the "motte-and-bailey" type. First, a motte (or mound) was raised to give the defensive structure height. Often, this could be accomplished by building on top of Roman ruins or a mountain. Then a wall surrounding an open area (the bailey, or keep) was built. Generally, the first such edifices of this kind were small towers, made of timber and earth. Inside the keep, makeshift shelter was arranged to suit man and beast. Sometimes a ditch, or moat, was dug around the wall to further discourage invasion. Gradually, as the need for hasty defense decreased, the towers were reinforced with stone. Eventually, all keeps were built of stone.

One of the first stone keeps of record is at Langeais in France, built in A.D. 994. Subsequent structures followed quickly. One of William the Conqueror's first acts was to build up fortresses such as the White Tower (commonly known as the Tower of London) immediately following the Conquest. Designed by a Norman monk named Gunulf, the original White Tower (c. 1074–97) was a classic motte-and-bailey keep. It was built of stone brought over from France, as if the Conqueror was unsure of England, distrusting its very firmament. Whatever the reason, the Tower of London has endured to this day, and remains the longest-standing, permanently held castle in Europe.

## The Motte-and-Bailey Castle

The motte-and-bailey castle originated in Byzantium, and became popular in the tenth century throughout Europe from Norman France to the Germanic and Slavic kingdoms. The Moslems first copied then perfected the towers of Byzantium in Spain, where they built elaborate fortresses from the early eighth to the late fifteenth centuries. These alcazares (derived from the Arabic word *al-quasir*, or castle) were situated in what is now Toledo, Segovia, Seville, and Granada.

**RIGHT:** The fifteenth-century Mazanareas El Real is the most elaborately decorated castle in Spain. Its towers are bossed with stone cannon balls and the machicolations are false, serving only an ornamental purpose.

**LEFT:** The Tower of London is among the oldest defensive structures in Europe, based on the "motte-and-bailey" plan adapted by the Normans from Byzantine models. The illustration depicts the captivity of the Duc d'Orléans following the Battle of Agincourt in 1415.

**FOLLOWING PAGE:** The Benedictine Abbey of Mont-St.-Michel in the Normandy region of France is surrounded by water at high tide. Founded in 708, it eventually became so strongly fortified that it withstood repeated English attacks during the Hundred Years War (1337–1453) without being captured.

Until the time of the Reconquest of Spain, when palatial fortresses such as the magnificent Alhambra were captured and the lessons of their architecture absorbed, castles were built exclusively to provide rough-and-ready defense. It was not until later that thought was given to a castle's comfort and suitability as living quarters; in fact, many castles were never intended as permanent dwellings.

But as the need to continuously occupy the structure arose, castles became more elaborate. Floors were added by gouging holes in the stone to support timber beams; fireplaces eventually replaced the open hearth. Private quarters, first for the lord, then for the lord's other family members, were constructed. The defenses too, became more elaborate; more baileys were added, surrounded by curtain walls. Wall walks were added for sentries; and openings known as arrow loops (later modified to accommodate rifles) were cut in the walls to better safeguard the defenders.

## The Crusades

The Crusades, a series of religious conquests, began in the eleventh century and continued into the fourteenth century. The main objective was to wrest the Holy Land from the infidel Seljuk Turks, who had suddenly claimed Jerusalem's citadel and were openly hostile to Christian pilgrim traffic.

Inspired by Pope Urban II and led by Europe's warrior princes, the first Crusade captured Antioch and Jerusalem in the late eleventh century and established a number of Crusader

**BELOW:** Looking through the arch of the drawbridge (main gate) of Carcassone, France, one sees the curtain wall and one of the principal towers in which the arrow slits are carefully placed to avoid weakening the masonry.

**RIGHT:** The citadel guarding the port of Antalya in western Turkey is noted for a wall that stretches for 5 miles (8 kilometers) along steep cliffs to protect against an attacking sea-borne enemy.

**LEFT:** The Alcazar in Segovia, Spain, was originally an Arab fortress dating from the eighth century, but was remodeled in the thirteenth century to be a royal residence of the Castilian kings. Gutted by fire in 1862, it has since been completely restored.

states. Also established at the beginning of the twelfth century were the Order of the Knights Hospitaler, the Order of Saint John of Jerusalem (1113), and the Knights Templar, or the Poor Fellow-Soldiers of Christ and the Temple of Solomon (1118). These orders played a crucial part in the refinement of castle design.

The second Crusade (1147–49) was less successful, and these Crusaders were forced to consolidate their power in an increasingly hostile territory. They did so by building more than a hundred castles in strategic areas throughout the Near East. In laying these defenses, more innovations in military architecture emerged, and these were different from the techniques being used in Europe.

The Crusaders reintroduced their motte-and-bailey architecture into the Near East, where it originated, and in turn absorbed the innovations that had occurred in their absence. The ruins of the great strongholds of the Crusades are found throughout the Near East. Among them are the castles of Krak

**ABOVE:** Though picturesque, these round gate towers with their machicolations could be deadly to any foe attacking Ponfernada, the Knights Templar castle in Spain.

**RIGHT:** The eleventh-century castle at Foix in France. Round towers had important advantages over square ones, offering a much wider field of fire to defenders and being more resistant to structural damage from battering rams and catapults.

**ABOVE:** The thick walls of Krak des Chevalier sheltered a
warren of living quarters, stables, and vast storage rooms that
could hold supplies sufficient to feed the castle's garrison for years.

**ABOVE:** One of the most famous castles of the Crusades, Krak des Chevaliers in Syria was secured by concentric fortifications in which each defensive position could cover the one beneath it. It was occupied by the Knights Hospitalers from 1109 until their final surrender in 1271.

des Chevaliers, Chastel Blanc, Château Pelerin, Margat, Monfort, and Saone.

Of these, Krak des Chevaliers in Syria is among the most well known and best preserved. It was a massive stronghold, built at the top of a mountain to guard the passes of the Mediterranean coast. Captured in 1099 in the early days of the first Crusade, Krak became a center for the Knights Hospitalers and contained lodging for their Grand Master. Fortified in the twelfth century with two encircling walls and a ditch that separated the walls from the castle, Krak remained in the Hospitalers' hold until its capture in 1271. After abandoning Krak, the Hospitalers removed themselves to Rhodes, where they retained their fortress until the sixteenth century.

The third Crusade (1188–92) is one of the most memorable. At this time, the brotherhoods of knights were in their prime, and the legendary European kings Richard I of England (Richard Coeur de Lion or Lionheart) and Phillip Augustus of France, were in the forefront.

The network of castles built at this time, which spread throughout Europe and the Middle East, guarded the supply lines of the Crusaders and their kingdoms at home. Among these, St. Hilarion and Château Gaillard were two of the most important, and both of these are intertwined with the legend of Richard Lionheart.

**LEFT:** Many-turreted Eltz Castle, on a promontory near the Moselle River in Germany, dates from the twelfth century. The castle's interior is divided into four separate living areas reflecting its shared, inherited ownership by four different families.

**LEFT:** The Blue Tower at Bad Wimpfen, Germany, is a twelfth-century structure built by the Emperor Frederick Barbarossa. It is surmounted by turrets from a later period.

**ABOVE:** The ill-fated castle standing high about the quaint town of Heidelberg is largely the work of sixteenth- and seventeenth-century builders. Its gutted interior and ruined corner tower resulted from a French attack in 1689 aimed at reducing German power.

## Coeur de Lion

Richard of England was not only an indefatigable Crusader but a tireless empire builder. By birth, he was king of England, where the nobility was truculent; and Duke of Normandy, where the French King Philip Augustus had designs on his property. He found the upkeep on his domains very costly and went on Crusade in part to find the money to maintain his supremacy.

Among other exploits, Richard founded the kingdom of Cyprus. Cyprus had been held by the Byzantine Empire since 965. In Cyprus, there was a monastery named St. Hilarion, after a local hermit who had fled the Holy Land. By the time the Normans arrived, St. Hilarion had already become well known for its defensive advantages. In the late eleventh century, the monastery was fortified against the attacking Seljuk Turks, probably at the instigation of the Byzantine Emperor Alexios I Comnemos (1081–1118). Not unlike many high places, the site of St. Hilarion had religious antecedents going back to pagan times; it was named Didymos (associated with the worship of Venus), which the Norman French eventually corrupted to Dieudamour.

However, Richard was able to seize Cyprus from the Byzantines in 1191, capturing Cyprus' governor, Isaac Comnemos. At first, Richard turned the island (along with Comnemos) over to the Knights Hospitalers for the total sum of 100,000 byzants—with 40,000 down. (A byzant was the gold coin of the Byzantine Empire, widely circulated throughout Europe during the middle ages.) The Hospitalers found themselves unable to hold the island, and returned it to Richard the following year. (Curiously, they retained Governor Comnemos until 1195.)

Lionheart, reluctant to part with the Hospitalers' deposit, bestowed Cyprus upon his noble countryman Guy de Lusignan, who thereby gained his own kingdom (after reimbursing the Hospitalers).

With hostilities heating up between the Lusignans and Frederick II of Spain, the monastery was converted into a fortress in the thirteenth century by the Lusignan regent, John d'Iberin. The fortress was a complicated division of three sections—the lower, middle, and upper wards. Ramparts were erected over the Byzantine foundations, and St. Hilarion became the principal stronghold of Cyprus.

The Lusignans ruled Cyprus from St. Hilarion for more than a century. Interestingly, throughout this militaristic phase of its history, St. Hilarion retained the relics of its monastic namesake, which an English traveler reported viewing as late as the fourteenth century.

With its ties to Norman Europe, Cyprus became a supply line to the Crusades and a center of trade in its own right. These supplies were often ferried by the Genoese and the Venetians, who in turn built many of the castles that are found throughout the Mediterranean today.

St. Hilarion was held by the Lusignans until the late fourteenth century, when the last Lusignan, Prince John of Antioch, was murdered by his mother, Queen Eleanor. The donjon—the inner tower or keep—at St. Hilarion is named after this unlucky prince, who, in a fit of paranoia, had dispatched his guard of mercenaries from its height.

Also associated with Richard I is the Château Gaillard in France. This château is considered the first great example of military architecture in Europe. Built around 1195 and situated near Rouen, the château presents an imposing crenellated outer wall to the Seine. The construction of Gaillard was costly, but

LEFT: Château Gaillard, the pride of Richard Coeur de Lion, was the acme of Norman defensive construction at the time of its construction in 1198. Gailliard included an unusual corrugated curtain wall in lieu of tower defenses, and had the first stone machicolations in Europe.

RIGHT: Richard Coeur de Lion, the greatest general of his age, is believed to have personally designed and supervised the building of Château Gailliard, since no architect is mentioned in the lists of expenses for the castle's construction.

Richard 1.st King of England
and Earl of Anjou

Duke of Normandy & Aquitaine
surnamed Coeur de Lion.

Richard deemed it worthwhile in order to consolidate his hold on his French domains. That, however, was not to be. In 1204, five years after Richard's death, the château succumbed to attack. This was accomplished by way of the château's latrine shaft, through which the invaders gained access.

Richard I was not the only king associated with Crusades and castle-building. Edward I (1239–1307) has also been recognized for his contributions in this area. His castles were considered "scientifically" designed, modeled as they were after the military architecture found in the Holy Land, which had withstood a great deal of aggression.

Edward built his castles along the English-Welsh border, in order to quell the frequent uprisings that occurred there. Among the first was Flint, with its classical rectangular bailey, moat, and circular donjon. Flint was followed by the castles of Harlech, Conway, and Caernarvon in 1282, which Edward began after there had been an uprising. These imposing structures did not intimidate the population as much as was desired, however, and Caernarvon was in fact damaged by another uprising about a dozen years later.

The castles of Caernarvon, Conway, and Flint, along with Aberystwyth and Rhuddlan, were attached to walled towns, and made great demands on the town economies, as did all castles. The building and sustaining of castles in general was costly, and nearby towns, the putative beneficiaries of the defenses, often bore the burden of debt.

Except when taking advantage of whatever natural defenses might have been available, Edward built his castles in concentric rings. Builth, Beaumaris, Aberystwyth, Harlech, and Rhuddlan all follow this pattern.

Another exemplary castle built in this time was Caerphilly Castle, built by one of the Earls of Gloucester between 1267–77. Edward's castles are said to share many similarities with this fortress.

## Walls as Defense

As a means of defense, manors, towns, and villages were often fortified with walls and ditches. In Spain, the fortification of cities was particularly sophisticated, due again to Moslem influence. The fortified towns of southern Spain, particularly

**RIGHT:** The gate at Carcassone, France, has close-set towers built with arrow slits and loopholes for bows and guns. The wall walk and one of the towers are shielded by wooden hoarding.

ABOVE: The medieval walled city of Carcassone, France, was protected by concentric fortifications. The town's castle is in the center foreground. Idyllic as it now seems, the strength (or lack thereof) of city walls spelled life or death for the community as frequent wars swept the region.

those of Cordoba, Granada, Malaga, Almeria, Toledo, and Zaragoza, combined military and civil architecture.

These Hispano-Arabic cities contained networks of walls in their fortified cities that could be taken as tangible expressions of their religious beliefs. The "true-believing" Christians were protected within the town's inner circle; the outcasts, "infidel" Jews and Moslems, were contained in ghettoes outside the city proper. Although they too had a similar network of walls protecting them, the Jews and Moslems also became, by their placement, the first line of defense for the Christian townspeople.

In West Africa, meanwhile, a great civilization had risen up independently of other influences. Discovered by the Portuguese traveler Joao Afonso de Aviero in the fifteenth century, the kingdom of Benin had existed for centuries before that. A curious network of earthwork walls, ramparts, and ditches encircles the site of the old kingdom. This network is said to have been built by the legendary Oba (King) Oguola in the thirteenth century, although it might have been built even earlier. The last of its moat-and-rampart structures is said to have been made by the Oba Ewuare in the fifteenth century; and this is closest to the center of the kingdom.

While it is agreed that this network comprises some sort of defense, it is unclear how this defense was effected. The wall sometimes ends on one side of its neighboring ditch, only to appear again on the other side. However, there are reports, dating from the early seventeenth century, claiming that dense forrestation protected the network.

In the Far East, China was often the progenitor of many types of defenses found elsewhere in Asia, not only because it was attacked many times by various hostile peoples but also because, it was a great civilization, predating others by centuries. In Korea, for example, a fortified wall known as the Cholli-Changsong—no doubt inspired by the Great Wall—has stood since the early eleventh century. The Cholli-Changsong stretched along the Manchurian border, protecting Korea from hostile invaders. Korean fortresses, too, were patterned after Chinese models. In the seventeenth century, fortifications such as the Namhan fortress with its 5-mile-long (8 kilometer) wall, were still considered effective. Korean cities were often walled. The walls surrounding the city of Songdo date from the early

**ABOVE:** Himeji Castle is a prime example of the castle-city favored by Japan's powerful feudal lords. It was built in the early seventeenth century; its name, meaning heron or egret, derives from the impressive white roofs of its dozens of buildings.

thirteenth century, and those that surrounded the old city of Seoul date from the early fifteenth century.

One of the most famous fortified cities in China is the Forbidden City, which until as late as 1911 was the home of the last rulers of China. Constructed in the early fifteenth century, the Forbidden City was not an actual city, but an enormous palatial enclave. The city's walls rise up to 35 feet (10.6 meters) high to enclose the palaces, shrines, halls, and gardens.

## The Castle Cities of Japan

During the period of European and Near Eastern history known as the middle ages, the far eastern lands of China, Korea, and Japan were united under the government of an emperor. It was a far from complacent relationship, however.

In China and Korea, separate states remained relatively stable under an imperial government. In Japan, leadership

decentralized around the twelfth century, giving way to powerful daimyos, or feudal barons, and did not reconsolidate until the Meiji Restoration in the late nineteenth century. Thus, the defenses and fortifications that were originally supposed to keep out foreign intruders were used against fellow Japanese. Following the emergence and rise of the shogunates in the early twelfth century, fortified mansions began to be built throughout Japan. Most of the castles standing today date from between 1480 and 1620, the most concentrated period of castle-building.

Many of these castles are masterpieces of civilian as well as military architecture. In its heyday, the castle was also the seat of the feudal lord, and as such reflected the Japanese esthetic preference for harmony with nature. Aspects of this can be seen in the way the outer stone walls of some Japanese castles are built in curved lines, which run parallel to eaves of the *tenshukaku*, or main tower. Additional towers, called *tsukimi* and *suzimi yagura*, used specifically for moon-viewing or other forms of nature meditation, also reflect this esthetic preference.

Early Japanese castles include Chihaya and Akasaka, built in 1330 by Masashige Kusunoki, the master architect of his day. The crowning achievement of Japanese military architecture was the perfection of the *tenshukaku*, which occurred during the Momoyama period (1570–1640), at the height of the daimyos' power. The *tenshukaku* was the command post from which all movements within and without the castle could be noted.

The perfection of the *tenshukaku* coincided with the refinement of the castle towns. The mighty lords of the Japanese medieval period built themselves castle cities, the center of which was the castle itself. Castles were no longer built exclusively on coasts and other rocky promontories but were also constructed upon flat land. Of the castles of this period, the most prominent that still stand today are Himeji and Matsuyama, both magnificent combinations of beauty and practicality. Himeji is often called the Castle of the Snowy Heron because of its white towers that rise up like a flock of birds.

**LEFT:** This nineteenth-century painting captures the chaos and violence of battle as Crusaders in the Holy Land defend their fortress against Muslim attackers. Of particular interest is the variety of weapons being used. The focal figure in red is the French knight William of Clermont.

**FOLLOWING PAGE:** Thirteenth-century Conway Castle, along with Caernavon and Harlech, was built by England's King Edward I to reinforce his control over Wales. Drawing on his experience in the Crusades, Edward situated his castles close to the shore so that both land and sea traffic could be observed and controlled.

**RIGHT:** Dornie Castle in the Scottish Highlands is an example of a fortified manor house, since there is no defensive wall. Perhaps the surrounding water and narrow bridge were thought to be sufficient protection.

**BELOW:** The thirteenth-century castle of Angers on the Loire River in France features a massive curtain wall joined to seventeen large, round towers with thickened bases. The plan of the fortress is an irregular pentagonal shape, and it contains no keep. The elaborate living quarters resembled a palace.

## Castles for the Middle Class

Between the late-thirteenth and early fourteenth centuries, the dispute of the Scottish succession led to clan feuds and generally opportunistic lawlessness, and this made the Scottish-English border a very dangerous place for the neighboring English villages. Thus, perhaps for the first time in history, the Crown encouraged its subjects near the border to erect the traditional perquisite of aristocracy—a castle—as a fortification of their living quarters.

Many of these border castles revived the single rectangular tower tradition that had been popular in the Norman style a century before, probably because it was easy to build and could be put up quickly.

Almost all towers had vaulted, fireproof basements, since being burned out was one of the most common dangers. And if time allowed, a stone wall enclosure, known as a barmkin, was built to conserve as much livestock as could be held.

As time went on, small landowners grew more expansive in their efforts to avoid wholesale destruction. Certain designs became popular, no doubt inspired by the real castles and fortified manors of the nobles. These were known as peles, or palisades, and bastels, or strong stone houses. Since their inhabitants had fewer resources than nobles, they met with less success in surviving the occasional siege. Middle-class castle-building continued up to the sixteenth century, when lawlessness had abated and the Crown once again frowned upon private fortifications.

**ABOVE:** Kesok Castle of Denmark, like many others in the Baltic
region, is constructed entirely of brick. Its plan includes a round
tower complete with a pepperpot roof at each corner of the structure.

## Plotting Destruction

Weapons technology had advanced roughly in a parallel trajectory with strategic sophistication ever since the first defensive wall had been erected. The ancient Greeks and Romans had used ballistic weaponry, battering rams, and siege towers in the attack of cities. By the twelfth century, the Arabs were using incendiary grenades, made of mud and bitumen, in their attacks. In the thirteenth century, the crossbow, a descendant of the antique ballista, made its appearance, with deadly power.

While many types of castle-breaching weapons evolved as a response to the design of fortifications, none had more effect than firearms. When the power of gunpowder was first discovered and employed in the fourteenth century, the reign of the castle began its decline.

In the fifteenth and sixteenth centuries, as artillery and other weaponry became more powerful and accurate, the great minds of the Renaissance—including Machiavelli, Leonardo da Vinci, and Michelangelo—were giving thought to innovative weapons of destruction. In fact, these men were once more esteemed for their contributions to military engineering than for their other artistic creations.

One major defensive innovation again came from Moorish-Christian Spain. In the twelfth and thirteenth centuries, the square towers of the Hispano-Arabic castles were modified into

**RIGHT:** The Alhambra, near Granada, Spain, is among the most impressive alcazars wrested from the Moors during the Christian Reconquest of the late fifteenth century. Built into the promontory of the Monte de Asabica, this combination of stronghold and palace is the finest example of Moorish architecture in Spain.

**LEFT:** Bodiam Castle in Sussex, England, is a fourteenth-century fortress built around a central court. Its gatehouse was stoutly defended by three portcullises, three gates, and a vaulted ceiling containing murder holes. It was never besieged.

**ABOVE:** Pfalzgrafenstein stands on an island in the Rhine River near Kaub, Germany. Begun in 1327 by Ludwig of Bavaria to serve as a toll station, it is notable for its hexagonal plan. The baroque roof of the central tower was added in the seventeenth century.

pentagonal ones. These alabarans became the forerunners of the fifteenth-century *torrioni* (as employed by Francesco Giorgio di Martini), which in turn begat the bastions employed by Antonio San Gallo and Michel San Michele.

These bastions were the first distinctive attributes of sixteenth-century papal fortresses. From then on, bastions became a standard feature of all European fortifications. As developed by San Michele and the San Gallo family, they were also refined and employed in defensive structures throughout the New World.

Military architects, including Pedro Luis Scrive, who built San Telmo Castle in Naples, were much sought after and could expect to find themselves fabulously paid and dispatched throughout the world. In the late fifteenth century, Italian architects working for the Grand Duke Ivan III were remodeling the defenses of the Moscow Kremlin. Also about that time, engineers of the Antonelli family were employed by the kings of Spain to lay out defenses for their far-flung empire.

**LEFT:** In the past, the defensive heart of every Russian city was its kremlin, which was an administrative and religious center as well as a refuge from attack. The most famous of these structures is the Moscow Kremlin, which dates in its present form from the fifteenth century.

**BELOW:** The castle at Haarzuilens dates from the fifteenth century. Damaged by fire in the last century, it was restored to pristine condition by the Rothschilds. Three hundred Dutch castles, out of two thousand built, still stand; these are mostly made of brick.

**RIGHT:** As defensive design improved, more efficient siege engines were developed. The attack tower dates to antiquity, but this early sixteenth-century Italian version attempts a new variation on an old theme.

## The Waning of Castles

By the seventeenth century, the castle had conspicuously lost favor as a serious means of defense. It could still be used, but cannon and other artillery were able to blast holes in and breach its once-sturdy walls.

Instead, castles began to serve other functions. Some, fitted with every affordable luxury, had become the permanent residences of royalty. Former donjons, such as the Louvre, were renovated and refined to the point that they became unrecognizable as castles and were used as palaces instead.

The White Tower, William the Conqueror's original Norman tower, became a royal prison as early as the thirteenth century; castles like Sudeley (which became the last home of Henry VIII's sixth wife, Katharine Parr) were also elaborated to include living quarters and eventually became royal palaces.

**ABOVE:** This painting by Canaletto of Alnwick Castle in northern England was made in the mid-eighteenth century. At this time, the ruins of medieval castles and abbeys were considered picturesque, and they inspired a taste for the Gothic that became part of the burgeoning Romantic movement.

Many of the seemingly timeless châteaux in France are relatively recent structures, built on the sites of former keeps. These include Pierre-en-Bresse, a late-seventeenth-century structure that rests on the foundations of an older, four-towered fortress. Fontaine-Francaise, constructed in 1750, is also built on top of a earlier fortress.

Many fortified structures built from the sixteenth century onward scarcely retain any remnants of their original military purpose. Included in these are the magnificent palaces of the Indian maharajahs—in particular the Palace of Man Singh I in Amber, India, with its beautiful gardens. Also among these are the "fantasy" castles built by Ludwig of Bavaria in the nineteenth century, for such structures were also meant to convey the sense of ease and luxury that political stability (often illusory) enjoyed by the nobility.

Other structures, having been ineffective in keeping people out, were later deployed to keep people in. One of these is the famous Bastille, a castle dating from the late fourteenth century,

whose prisoners included such notables as Voltaire and the Marquis de Sade. The supposedly inhuman uses to which the Bastille had been put so infuriated the Parisian populace that their ransacking of it during the French Revolution (July 14, 1789) is commemorated to this day.

Castles in general were also defeated by the rise of unified governments throughout the world. The kings of nations began to destroy or encourage their destruction in the event of a civilian war. In Spain, such destruction began with the consolidation of Aragon and Castile and the Reconquest, which was completed in 1492.

In Japan, castle destruction began in the seventeenth century with the Tokugawa dictatorship (1640–1869), and lasted until the Meiji Restoration. At that time, the Japanese eschewed their traditional designs in favor of the European bastion, and began lining their coasts with fortifications against invasion. Goryokaku Castle, in Hokkaido, is an example of this European-influenced design.

**LEFT:** Agra Fort in India is a seventeenth-century stronghold begun by the Mogul conqueror Akbar (1542–1605) and completed by his grandson. The fortress complex is triangular in shape, with surrounding walls that are 1.5 miles (2.4 kilometers) long and almost 70 feet (21.3 meters) high. It was a residential fortress and administrative seat.

**LEFT:** Muiden Castle, on the confluences of the Vecht and Ijssel rivers (near Amsterdam in the Netherlands) was built by Albert of Bavaria between 1370 and 1386. A typical castle of the "square" plan, Muiden's red brick restoration occurred much later.

**RIGHT:** In this illustration, the Bastille looms large as the symbol of royal oppression. The structure, dating from the fourteenth century, was attacked by a revolutionary mob on July 14, 1789. Shortly thereafter, it was demolished. Throughout France, castles became associated with the feudalism that the Revolution was trying to abolish.

**BELOW:** The plan of horseshoe-shaped towers attached to a circular wall was designed to resist gunfire. The three towers of Beersel Castle in Belgium were added in 1491 to already existing walls.

By the eighteenth century, a spirit of romantic morbidity had settled on Europe. Castles, with their often gloomy history, became favorite settings for ghost stories. Legends of haunted castles became popular (and remain so today), and centuries-old stories of the "little princes in the Tower" and mysterious deaths at Kenilworth and other atrocities were all the rage. Glamis Castle in Scotland, which first reached the popular imagination as the setting for Shakespeare's *Macbeth*, has acquired even more notoriety since then; and the story of the three cartloads of human bones unearthed from an old oubliette at Leap Castle in Ireland in the nineteenth century is enough to give anyone nightmares.

By the late eighteenth century, the popularity of castles as the haunts of both spirits and history caused many of them to be acquired and renovated according to the tastes of the times. Glen Castle in Ireland, for example, originally a fourteenth-century castle, was "restored" to Georgian Gothic in 1789. In France, Commarin, a fifteenth-century castle, has eighteenth-century modifications but retains its fifteenth-century chapel and four corner towers.

The deployment of traditional fortifications was fast becoming useless; artillery was sophisticated and powerful enough to blast a hole in any wall. And in areas where artillery was less sophisticated, there were always the traditional methods of siege.

**BELOW:** At Lake Garda near the Swiss border stands the Castle of Sermione, Italy. The towers have deep crenellations, surmounted by a chevron design made of bricks.

**LEFT:** Satzvey Castle in Germany is a fifteenth-century structure that was renovated in the nineteenth century. Although no longer completely genuine, its massive gatehouse and watery location help the complex to retain a medieval aura.

**RIGHT:** This reconstruction of a fourteenth-century kitchen at Kreuzenstein Castle in Austria shows the type of space and equipment used to feed a large household. Of special interest is the covered cooking area at the left, with its array of heavy vessels.

**LEFT:** Standing on an island in Lake Geneva that has been fortified since ancient times, the thirteenth-century castle of Chillon was used mainly to control shipping on the lake. Its strongest defense, three rounds towers and a square corner tower, face the land side of the island.

**RIGHT:** A reception hall in Chillon Castle on Lake Geneva. Castle interiors were often far from gloomy, decorated as they were with brightly painted designs and even scenes from folktales and biblical stories.

# CHAPTER THREE

# THE NEW WORLD

$A$t the time when the kingdoms and empires of the Old World were arranging themselves to become the body of nations of the modern day, a different struggle was going on in the New World. Once its discovery was credited to the European navigator Christopher Columbus on behalf of Spain, all the nations of Europe were eager to exploit the find.

This jockeying for mastery was attempted on two levels: the traditional appropriation of territory in the name of a king or emperor; and the newer, mercantile technique of licensing and exploiting a region's resources for fledgling capitalism. Both of these forces were responsible for the building of fortifications in the New World.

In their comparatively short history, the fortifications of the New World have seen a great deal of action. Their first purpose was to guard new European settlements against often hostile indigenous populations. In later years, however, as those European settlements strengthened and grew into prosperous colonies, they would often turn upon each other, and fortifications became prizes in a seemingly endless fight for supremacy.

Like medieval castles and their ghosts, some New World fortifications hold ugly memories. At the notorious Castillo de San Carlos de Cabana in Havana, Cuba, for example, a wall is pock-marked with bullet holes in a line 100 feet (30.5 meters) long. It is said that political prisoners were taken there to be shot without trial.

**LEFT:** Fort Wood, built in a star shape, defended New York harbor for most of the nineteenth century until it became the base for the Statue of Liberty in the 1880s.

## Stronghold of the Conquistadors

The Spanish, who first discovered the New World, were the first to take advantage of the opportunities they found. The need to defend their territory prompted them to build the principal strongholds of the Americas, which lined the seacoasts and waterways.

The Spanish had refined the notions of bastioned fortresses and built many long-lasting stone structures. Among the legendary Spanish fortresses, many of the earliest and best preserved are to be found on the coastlines and islands of the Caribbean and Florida. These include the historic castles of Havana's harbor, Castillo de la Fuerza and Castillo de San Carlos de Cabana; Castillo de San Felipe del Morro (called El Morro), protecting the harbor of San Juan, Puerto Rico; and San Marcos at St. Augustine, Florida, the oldest fortress of its kind in the United States.

Legendary explorer-conquistador Hernando de Soto directed the construction of La Fuerza in the early sixteenth century. La Fuerza is considered to be one of the oldest fortresses of western design in the New World. It was also considered an important stronghold from the first, and by 1544 was to be "saluted" by all marine traffic passing through Havana's harbor. De Soto departed shortly after its construction to explore North America, and, in true medieval tradition, he left the castle's management to his wife, Isabel de Bobadilla, who did not see her husband again for four years.

The Castillo de la Fuerza was of quadrangular construction, with a bastion at each of its corners. Its double walls were 25 feet (7.6 meters) high, and it was encircled by a ditch. One entered La Fuerza by means of a plank walk, which was later replaced by a drawbridge.

**ABOVE:** Situated high above the entrance to the harbor of San Juan, Puerto Rico, "El Morro" Castle is an example of "defense-in-depth." More sophisticated than concentric defensive structures, the fort was built in a prickly star pattern that is extremely difficult to breach.

**RIGHT:** El Morro was begun in 1539 and was constantly improved over the centuries. A later addition, the Santa Barbara battery, is noted for its thick walls as demonstrated by the strongly protected stairway shown here.

In the latter part of the sixteenth century, because of the piratical threat posed by Sir Francis Drake, La Fuerza was joined in the Caribbean region by the famous fortress El Morro as well as by the Castle of the Three Kings and La Punta. All three were begun in 1589 and completed in 1597.

El Morro was an imposing structure from the first. Rising more than 100 feet (30.5 meters) from the sea at the mouth of San Juan harbor, its design showed the continuing influence of Moorish architecture on Spain. The foundations of El Morro rested upon rock, and a road leading to the castle had to be carved out of the same rock. El Morro had a battery of twelve guns on its ramparts, which were known, in the mordant humor of the time, as the Twelve Apostles.

With its extensive fortifications, Havana was deemed sufficiently protected from foreign intrusion. In spite of this, the city fell to English attack nearly two hundred years later, in 1762. Following Havana's reinstatement as a Spanish colony the following year, a new fortress was begun to protect the city. The enormous Castillo de San Carlos de Cabanas, nearly 1 mile (1.609 kilometers) in length and about a fifth of a mile wide, was built at the almost incredible cost of $14 million. The amount of money spent on San Carlos—though extraordinary—must be seen in light of the fortunes made by both the conquistadors and the Spanish Crown in exploiting the New World. Havana was one of its greatest ports. For that reason, the Crown was willing to spend money not only on

San Carlos, but also on the castles of Principe (1774) and Atares (1767)—and on others throughout New Spain—in order to protect its investment.

Among other Spanish strongholds were castles built on the Florida mainland. These include San Marcos (1672), San Carlos de Barrancas (c.1699), and Matanzas (1740).

BELOW: The massive walls of Castillo de San Cristobal in San Juan were made necessary by the development of cannon that fired more damaging elongated projectiles instead of cannonballs.

RIGHT: An overhead view of the gun emplacements at El Morro. Heavy cannon were able to swivel on embedded tracks and fire through embrasures angled to enable guns to follow a moving target.

LEFT: Built in 1672, the Castillo de San Marcos at St. Augustine, Florida, is the oldest existing seacoast fort in the United States.

**ABOVE:** The Castillo de San Marcos is built of coquina and lime, a combination resistant to gunfire. It follows the plan of a central court surrounded by a tall, thick wall with arrow-shaped bastions.

**RIGHT:** The combination of walls with corner bastions makes Castillo de San Marcos a large gun platform from which every square foot of wall can produce cannon fire.

Castillo de San Marcos at St. Augustine is the oldest stone fortification in the United States. It guarded one of Spain's oldest settlements in North America, which was often menaced by local tribes, as well as the English settlements in Georgia to the north.

Although built out of the local coquina (limestone), San Marcos strongly resembles the fortresses of Europe, with its high, thick walls and moat. It was strong enough to withstand numerous sieges, and wasn't defeated until 1862, during the American Civil War, when many modern forts were faring worse.

Near San Marcos, on an island 14 miles (22.5 kilometers) south of Saint Augustine, stands the quadrangular stone Fort Matanzas. The fortress was begun in 1740, and employed convict labor, which—along with slavery and peonage—was a popular New World source for labor. It took two years to complete, due to the hazards of the island's shifting sands.

Fort San Carlos de Barrancas, which is in Pensacola, Florida, was built sometime before 1699. It was a semicircular fortress guarding the bay. Unlike San Marcos or Matanzas, San Carlos did not have a very successful martial history; the Spanish surrendered it to the French in 1719 only to regain it by treaty in 1720. After 1763, San Carlos passed repeatedly back and forth between the Spanish and the English, who blew it up during the War of 1812.

All Spanish territories in Florida were ceded to the United States in 1821. Except for hostilities during the Civil War, they were not used after that and they have been part of the United States national park system since the early years of this century.

## The Fight for North America

The Spanish had, to a degree, bequeathed the greater part of North America to whomever wished to claim it. By the seventeenth century, these claimants included the French, who had settled Canada and the waterways of North America; the Dutch, who had established a prosperous settlement in New York harbor; and the English, who more ambitiously and with varying degrees of success, had settled the Atlantic coastline from Nova Scotia to Georgia.

In the beginning, humble forts and wooden stockades were erected by all three of these groups to guard against the predations of hostile indigenous tribes. While this threat became more real as the frontier continued to move west, the danger of attack in the east came increasingly from fellow Europeans. For these and other reasons, the defenses of the settlements began to be more elaborate.

One of the most illustrious fortifications in North America is Castle St. Louis, built in 1608 along the St. Lawrence River in Quebec, Canada. Originally consisting of little more than gun platforms, Castle St. Louis withstood numerous British sieges

LEFT: Fort Jefferson, in the Dry Tortugas Islands, Florida, was designed to protect an important anchorage in the Gulf of Mexico with its 450 guns. Its plan is hexagonal, with two tiers of casemates, bastions, and a moat.

**ABOVE:** The combination of palisade and blockhouse was common on the North American frontier. However, these defenses often could not resist a determined attack, as shown in this depiction of the massacre at Fort Mims in 1813.

by gradually evolving over the course of one hundred years into a formidable fortress. But that time, however, its purpose was nearly at an end.

Castle St. Louis was originally established by Samuel de Champlain (c. 1567–1635), who also founded the Quebec settlement in "New France." It was, however, de Montmagny (who was, coincidentally, a Knight of Malta), who rebuilt it

in stone around 1636. The castle was further strengthened and enlarged by the military architect Sebastien de Vauban under the direction of the Comte de Frontenac et Palluau later in the seventeenth century. It was shortly after this that the now-famous Citadel, the pinnacle of which is known as the King's Bastion, was erected in 1720. The Citadel rises 350 feet (106.7 meters) from the St. Lawrence River, and commands an imposing view of the city.

Quebec fell to the British in 1759, during the French and Indian War (1754–63). This conflict necessitated the building of many defenses along the waterways that now form the United States–Canadian border—where the French had trading outposts, as well as in major port cities elsewhere in the United

**ABOVE:** Fort King George at Darien, Georgia, dates from 1741. The American colonists, though familiar with European fortress design, were limited by scarce resources and manpower. However modest, this frontier fort is protected by a moat, a timber wall or palisade, and a wooden blockhouse that functioned as a keep.

**LEFT:** In this detail of a reconstructed battery at Fort Lee, New Jersey, can be seen a wall of fascenes, bundles of long, rod-like sticks that served as a buffer against gunfire. Defenses of this kind could be repaired or strengthened with materials from surrounding woodlands.

States. Among these are the historical sites of Fort Niagara and Ticonderoga (in northern New York State), Fort Duquesne (in Pittsburgh, Pennsylvania), and the "lost fort" of Fort Charlotte, near Mobile, Alabama. Each of these forts was strategically important in the fight among the European forces for the New World.

Fort Niagara, on the Niagara River at Lake Ontario, was one of the first stone forts built by the French to safeguard their fur trapping industry. It was completed in 1726. In 1759, it was captured by the British during the French and Indian War. After that Fort Niagara passed between British and American hands at least twice between 1796 and 1815.

Ticonderoga was a stone fort situated between Lake Champlain and Lake George. Built by the French in 1755 at the onset of the French and Indian War (1754–63), Ticonderoga almost immediately became the focus of British enmity.

The British wrested Ticonderoga from the French in 1759, marking the fort's end as a French outpost. Later, during the American Revolution, Ticonderoga became an object of conquest for both the British and colonial forces. It became an American fort with the cessation of hostilities.

Almost simultaneously with the construction of Ticonderoga, the French built Fort Duquesne on the confluence of the Allegheny and Monongahela rivers in 1754. It remained in French hands until November of 1758, when it was abandoned in the face of advancing British forces.

One fort in particular illustrates the shifting lines of territorial claims that were common to early American history. In 1704, the French built a stockade fort of cedarwood near present-day Mobile, Alabama. Originally Fort Louis de la Mobile, it was renamed Fort Conde in 1711. During the French and Indian War, in 1863, the British captured Fort Conde, renaming it Fort Charlotte. Fort Charlotte remained in British hands until 1780, when it was seized by Bernardo de Galvez, the Spanish governor of Louisiana. Finally, the fort was surrendered to the Americans in 1813, during the War of 1812. In 1820, it was destroyed outright.

**RIGHT:** Like many fortresses along what is now the United States–Canadian border, Fort Ticonderoga was much contested between the English, the French, and the Colonials. Originally a stone fort built by the French in 1755 and based on continental models, it has been rebuilt in the twentieth century.

## From Revolution to Civil War

From the onslaught of the American Revolution (1776–84) to the end of the Civil War (1862–65), the fledgling nation of the United States was forged. During this time, existing fortifications would demonstrate over and over again the flaws of their almost medieval simplicity.

During the American Revolution, hostilities were mostly confined to those between the British and the colonials, although—as in the case of unlucky Fort Charlotte—other nations might jump in where an opportunity for land-grabbing presented itself. The War of 1812 was an acknowledged free-for-all; one might even say that it was a precursor to the world wars of the twentieth century. During this time, fortifications throughout the New World were seeing a fair share of activity. When Fort McHenry, built in 1799 to defend Baltimore harbor, was being heavily bombarded by a British fleet, the incendiary incident led Francis Scott Key, a prisoner of war, to pen "The Star-Spangled Banner."

**ABOVE:** During the War of 1812, the pentagonal brick design of Fort McHenry, Maryland, was able to withstand artillery fire from sixteen British warships in Baltimore harbor, inspiring Francis Scott Key's poem "The Star-Spangled Banner."

Between each conflict, fortifications were being built or restored. Each conflict, however, exposed new weaknesses in the fortifications. One conflict in particular, occurring long after the War of 1812 had ended, tested fortifications to the limits—the attack on Fort Sumter that began the Civil War.

Fort Sumter, a pentagonal brick fort situated on an island in Charleston harbor in South Carolina, sustained a thirty-four-hour siege before its commander, Major Robert Anderson, surrendered on April 14, 1861.

The fort became a point of honor for both sides as they strove for mastery during the four-year conflict. The Confederate army paid dearly for its preemptive strike as Fort Sumter, which had become a Union objective, underwent a fifteen-month siege from 1863 to 1864. Finally, the fort was evacuated in 1865 with the approach of the Union army.

**ABOVE:** Fort Sumter, built in 1829 to protect the harbor and city of Charleston, South Carolina, was heavily damaged by artillery fire from a Confederate battery on the night of April 12–13, 1861. This marked not only the beginning of the American Civil War but the decline of fortifications of this type.

**ABOVE:** Shown here in a contemporary photograph is the debris
and destruction caused by the twenty-nine-hour bombardment
of Confederate-held Fort Pulaski by Federal forces in 1862.

In 1862, the Union army bombarded Fort Pulaski, near Savannah, Georgia, for about twenty-nine hours. Built in 1831, Fort Pulaski was constructed of bricks at a cost of one million dollars. At the time of its construction, it was considered one of the great forts of its kind. The fort had gun casemates on three sides. It also had narrow openings for rifle fire and an encircling moat—defensive features dating back to the middle ages.

The destruction of Forts Sumter and Pulaski proved that these brick coastal fortifications, which were begun following the War of 1812, had already been rendered obsolete by innovations in ordnance. Fort Pulaski was abandoned as a fortification after the Civil War. Damage done by the Confederate and Union artillery may be still be viewed at both forts, which have been restored and designated historic monuments.

**ABOVE:** Fort Fisher, North Carolina, was an earthwork fortification armed with heavy swiveling cannon. The example shown here is mounted on a typical wooden gun carriage of the era, which was easy and inexpensive to manufacture. Note the long horizontal tracks that allow the gun to recoil when fired.

**FOLLOWING PAGE:** Casemate emplacements of cannon at Fort Pulaski, Georgia, provided a bomb-proof roof supported by masonry arches to protect the guns. Built as a state-of-the-art fort in 1847, it proved no match to the increased firepower developed in the following decades.

**RIGHT:** This is a reconstruction of the fortified town of Boonesboro, Kentucky, built by Daniel Boone in 1775. The elevated back walls of private houses served as the fort's defensive walls. Blockhouses at each corner provide added security. In spite of these measures, Boonesboro was eventually abandoned because of repeated attacks by Native Americans.

## Westward Bound

But if fortifications were becoming obsolete in the East, they were still reasonably effective along the western frontier, where hostile forces had less access to sophisticated weaponry. Hostility could be fierce when it occurred, and woe to anyone who could not gain the safety of the fort. The following is an account of an Indian attack near Chicago in 1812:

> A corporal and six soldiers had gone up the river to fish. . . . When the fishing party reached "Lee's place," it was proposed to stop and bid the inmates to be on their guard, as the signal from the fort indicated danger. All was still around the house, but they groped their way, and as the corporal leaped the fence into the small enclosure, he placed his hand upon the dead body of a man, who he soon ascertained had been scalped . . . It was subsequently ascertained, from traders in the Indian country, that the perpetrators of this bloody deed were a party of Winnebagoes, who had come into the neighborhood determined to kill every white man without the walls of the fort.

This fort is typical of those found elsewhere in the country at the time, possessing the elements of classic fortifications and also taking advantage of whatever natural defenses were present. It was "constructed with two blockhouses on the southern side, and a sallyport or subterranean passage from the parade-ground to the river, designed either to facilitate escape, or as a means of supplying the garrison with water during a siege."

As one traveled farther west, one could see more and more forts that were constructed by civilians, such as the famous Fort Laramie in the Wyoming Territory. Originally called Fort William (after one of its founders, a fur trapper), Fort Laramie was constructed as a square fort in 1834. It was fenced by pickets 18 feet (5.5 meters) high, with two bastions at diagonally opposite corners. In 1836, the American Fur Company undertook the refurbishment of Fort Laramie, making it into an oblong fort at a cost of $10,000. The new fort had adobe walls 15 feet (4.5 meters) high, with clay bastions and a slender palisade for patrolling. There was one entrance with two gates in order to maintain security. The inside of the fort was divided into a public "square" with offices and a protected area for sheltering animals in case of Indian attack.

In 1849 the United States government bought Fort Laramie from the American Fur Company, probably for fifty cents on the dollar. The purpose of the fort from then on was to protect wagon trains on the Wyoming Trail. In 1854, a company of officers rode out to investigate a complaint made by a Mormon wagon train; the soldiers were massacred by the Sioux. The fort was eventually closed when it was bypassed by the train line.

Hostilities between European settlers and Native Americans were nearly always territorial disputes. One of the bloodiest of these occurred near Fort Kearney, situated in the northern Rocky Mountains. Fort Kearney was a typical fort of its time—a stockade with a parade ground, covering four acres, that guarded the Bozeman Trail (a branch of the Oregon Trail). In 1866, it was the site of the Fetterman Massacre, where a company of eighty soldiers, led by a hot-blooded captain of the same name, was ambushed and slaughtered by two thousand Native Americans led by the famed warriors Crazy Horse and Red Cloud. The massacre (which Fetterman survived) led to a treaty with the Sioux. Fort Kearney was abandoned two years later; shortly after, the Sioux burned it down completely.

Another western outpost, Fort Union in New Mexico, helped administer supplies along the Sante Fe Trail. Although spartan by today's standards, Fort Union must have been a welcome sight after a long trek through hostile territory. The fort had storehouses, a commissary, and a hospital that also functioned as a hospice, letting beds for fifty cents a night.

## Remember the Alamo

In the annals of American history, the Texas fight for independence against Spain (1835–36) looms as large as any battle of the American Revolution, the Civil War, or even the winning of the American West. A struggle of courage against overwhelming odds, it is associated with two American legends, Davy Crockett and Jim Bowie.

The Alamo structure itself, a quadrangular fort with a central court, was originally built in 1744 as a chapel attached to a Franciscan mission. It was later converted into a small garrison fort for the purpose of housing Spanish troops. Therefore, it is

**LEFT:** Here, some of the 150 defenders of the Alamo fire across the walls at the Mexican Army in 1836. For almost two weeks the small force held out until it was overwhelmed.

ironic that, in 1836, a small troop of Americans were able to use the Alamo to their advantage, holding off the Mexican army of Antonio Lopez de Santa Anna for almost two weeks.

All the defenders of the Alamo lost their lives in the siege. Their selfless act so hampered the actions of Santa Anna that he was ultimately defeated. The incident became an inspiration to the fledgling nation of Texas, which became a state in 1845. The Alamo fort, which was severely damaged in the battle, has been lovingly preserved to this day.

## The End of an Era

In the United States, the use of forts had basically ended with the taming of the West. In the Spanish-American War (1898), the last major military engagement of the United States in the Americas, forts and military posts were used to launch armies and ships to their point of engagement.

Ironically, among the military outposts engaged in the conflict was the Presidio, an outpost that had been established by Spain in 1776 to protect its young settlement at San Francisco. The Presidio of San Francisco was at the time the most important military site in the West, and its post, Fort Winfield Scott, had been built at a cost of two million dollars.

The Presidio was a point of departure for the Philippines during the Spanish-American War. (As in the case of the Alamo, a fortification that had been built by the Spanish colonials was again being used against them.) Like many former forts, much of the Presidio is now a national park.

Among other sites important to early American history that have been turned into parks are Ticonderoga and Forts Niagara and Stanwix, all of which are in New York State. It has been necessary to restore many of the old forts; Fort Stanwix, in fact, was completely restored from old records in honor of the nation's Bicentennial in 1976. Of interest to Civil War enthusiasts are the many forts involved in this conflict that have been preserved, including the famous Forts Sumter and Moultrie in Charleston Harbor and Forts Frederica and Pulaski along the Georgia coast.

**RIGHT:** The Alamo was originally a mission chapel but was modified for use by a Spanish garrison. Though not unusual in design, its fame was established in 1836 when a small band of Texas independence fighters were able, for a time, to stave off the advance of the Mexican Army.

# AFTERWORD

$F$*in de siècle*—the phrase used to describe the end of the last century—could also be used to describe the end of the age of castles. At the close of the nineteenth century, the world was changing. For some time, the emphasis in military engineering had been moving away from fixed fortifications such as castles and forts and moving toward more mobile means of defense, such as ironclad battleships, armored cars, and tanks.

## New Ways of Warfare

The moment of truth for fixed fortifications came in 1914, when the "Great War" commenced and warfare changed forever. Fortifications were now "constructed" by digging ditches and firing one's guns from there. Aerial assault, first by zeppelin, then by plane, completely eliminated castles as tactical defenses, and once impregnable castles regularly became the helpless targets of aerial aggression. Many Spanish castles and historical fortifications came to harm in the Spanish Civil War.

During World War II, the point was driven home, as once again castles—as well as the towns and cities they once protected—suffered helplessly in the wake of hostilities. Scathed by war were France (including Normandy, home of William the Conqueror), Belgium, Germany, and Austria.

The Second World War also impacted the historic castles of Japan. Approximately three hundred of the estimated five thousand castles built in Japan's history were still standing in the nineteenth century, but by the end of World War II only fifty remained. Among the sites where castles were bombed are Sendai, Nagoya, Ogaki, Wakayama, Okayama, Hiroshima, and Fukuyama.

## Castles in the Present Day

In spite of the ravages of time, thousands of castles remain standing today. Some of these, such as the venerable and remote Crusader castles of the twelfth and fifteenth centuries, are mere shells, visited by the occasional adventurous traveler. Some, like the glorious Tower of London in England, or the Louvre in Paris, are well-preserved museums visited by thousands of tourists every year.

Very few castles have remained in the hands of the original owners, or even in private hands. Among the few is Muncester Castle in England, which has been the home of the Pennington

family since the time of Henry VI (1421–71). Many castles, including Muncester, are in the service of and are also preserved by the state. Included among these are Bratislava Castle in the Slovak Republic (now serving as an official state residence), Rosendael in the Netherlands, and the many French châteaux that are under the protection of the Historic Monuments Service. In addition, many private organizations, both national and international, are dedicated to preserving the castle's heritage.

Literally hundreds of thousands of castles remain throughout the world to this day, and it is an enduring testament to the strength of castles and similar fortifications that, having been in decline for so long, there are so many still standing. The ruins of mighty walls dating from many centuries ago and the structures of the ancient Greeks and Romans have successfully resisted obscurity. That they continue to survive is a monument to the people who built them.

# GLOSSARY

**Alcazar.** A castle or fortress of the Spanish Moors

**Bailey.** The courtyard of a castle

**Bastion.** The projecting portion of a fortification that is attached to the main structure at its base

**Battery.** A fortified position equipped with artillery

**Battlement.** A defensive or decorative parapet

**Blockhouse.** A building, usually wooden, having a projecting upper story with loopholes for firearms

**Casemate.** A strongly-built vault or chamber for the protection of an artillery piece with an embrasure, often armored, through which the gun can fire

**Concentric Fortification.** A design in which two or more circles of walls form the defensive plan

**Crenels.** The open spaces between the merlons of a battlement

**Curtain Wall.** A wall that encloses the courtyard of a castle, generally connecting the towers or bastions

**Donjon.** The keep of a castle

**Embrasure.** An opening through which missiles may be discharged or guns fired

**Keep.** The chief tower of a castle

**Loopholes.** Slits in fortifications through which arrows may be fired

**Machicolation.** An opening or series of openings in the tops of walls through which liquids and projectiles could be thrown

**Merlon.** The solid portion of a battlement (in which merlons alternate with crenels to form a defensive parapet)

**Moat.** A deep ditch, filled with water, that surrounds a castle or stronghold

**Motte.** A raised mound, natural or manmade, on which the tower of a fortification is constructed

**Murder Holes.** An opening over a door or other entrance used to fired upon intruders

**Oubliette.** A secret dungeon with a trap-door opening only in the ceiling, as found in certain old castles

**Palisade.** A defensive wall of stakes or timbers set into the ground (also called a stockade)

**Portcullis.** A strong grating, often made of iron, which may be lowered in the passageway of a castle to prevent entrance or exit from the premises.

**Rampart.** A defensive wall, usually of packed earth capped with a stone or earth parapet, that surrounds a fortification

**Stockade.** An enclosure constructed of stakes or posts fixed in the ground that forms a defensive barrier against attack

**Turret.** A small tower, usually at the angle of the building, forming a part of the larger structure of a castle or fortress

# INDEX